REEL WOMEN

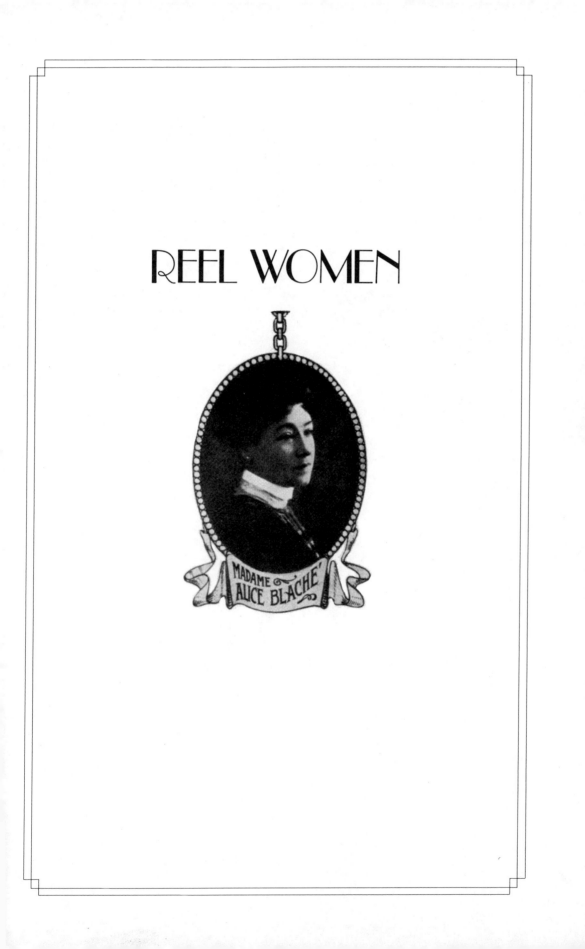

MADAME ALICE BLACHÉ

ALLY ACKER

REEL WOMEN

PIONEERS OF THE CINEMA
1896 TO THE PRESENT

◆

Foreword by *JUDITH CRIST*

Afterword by *MARC WANAMAKER*

B. T. Batsford Ltd, London

This edition first published in the United States by
The Continuum Publishing Company
370 Lexington Avenue, New York, NY 10017
and in Great Britain by
B. T. Batsford, Ltd
4 Fitzhardinge Street, London W1H OAH

A catalogue record for this book is held at the British Library
ISBN 0 7134 6960 9

for my father,
mortimer acker (1920–1990),

without whom no portion
of the reel women book or films
could have been realized

for muggie, my wild swan,
in peace and freedom wherever you fly

for alana, some models for you
to follow

and for the women named
and unnamed in these pages
whose middle name is courage

here is my endless love letter to you

CONTENTS

◆ ◆ ◆

Acknowledgments xi
Foreword by Judith Crist xiv
Introduction—The Feminization of
Filmmaking xvii

I. ◆ **Reel Women Directors**

PREVIEW 3
THE SILENTS 7
ALICE GUY BLACHÉ (1875–1968) 7
LOIS WEBER (1882–1939) 12

SHORT TAKES 17
IDA MAY PARK (?–1954) 17
RUTH ANN BALDWIN (*) 18
ELIZABETH PICKETT (*) 19
MARGUERITE BERTSCH (?–1967) 20

THE SOUND ERA 21
DOROTHY ARZNER (1900–1979) 21
JOAN TEWKESBURY 29
CLAUDIA WEILL 31
JOAN MICKLIN SILVER 33
KAREN ARTHUR 35
MARTHA COOLIDGE 37
SUSAN SEIDELMAN 40
DONNA DEITCH 42

SHORT TAKES 45
JOYCE CHOPRA 45
STEPHANIE ROTHMAN 46

II. ◆ **Reel Women Actresses
Turned Director/
Producer**

PREVIEW 51
THE SILENTS 53
MARY PICKFORD (1893–1979) 53
MABEL NORMAND (1894–1930) 56
NELL SHIPMAN (1892–1970) 59
LILLIAN GISH (1896–   ) 62

SHORT TAKES 65
RUTH STONEHOUSE (1893–1941) 65
LUCILLE MCVEY (1890–1925) 67
LULE WARRENTON (1863–1932) 67
CLEO MADISON (1883–1964) 68
MARGERY WILSON (1898–1986) 70

THE SOUND ERA 74
IDA LUPINO (1918–   ) 74
BARBARA LODEN (1932–1980) 78
ELAINE MAY 81
LEE GRANT 84
BARBRA STREISAND 87
PENNY MARSHALL 89

III. ◆ **Reel Women
of the Avant-Garde**

PREVIEW 95
MAYA DEREN (1917–1961) 95

SHIRLEY CLARKE (1925–) 97
YVONNE RAINER 99

SHORT TAKES 102
MARIE MENKEN (1909–1970) 102
MARY ELLEN BUTE (1909–) 103

IV. ◆ Reel Women of Color

PREVIEW 110
THE MANDARIN FILM COMPANY 111
KATHLEEN COLLINS (1942–1988) 111
RITA MORENO 113
MAYA ANGELOU 116
EUZHAN PALCY 118
RUBY OLIVER 121
CHRISTINE CHOY 123
JULIE DASH 125

SHORT TAKES 127
PEACHES JONES (1952–1988) 127
MICHELLE PARKERSON 128
AYOKA CHENZIRA 129
SAUNDRA SHARP 130
ALILE SHARON LARKIN 131
MADELINE ANDERSON 132
ELOICE GIST 132
FRANCES WILLIAMS 132

V. ◆ Reel Women Producers

PREVIEW 135
VIRGINIA VAN UPP (1902–1970) 137
SHERRY LANSING 140
DAWN STEEL 143

SHORT TAKES 146
DOROTHY DAVENPORT REID (1895–1977) 146
FANCHON ROYER (1902–?) 149
HANNAH WEINSTEIN (1911–1984) 150
MARCIA NASATIR 151

VI. ◆ Reel Women Writers

PREVIEW 155
THE SILENTS 159
GENE GAUNTIER (1891–1966) 159
GRACE CUNARD (1893–1967) 161
JUNE MATHIS (1892–1927) 164
ELINOR GLYN (1864–1943) 166

*FROM THE SILENTS
  TO THE SOUND ERA* 171
FRANCES MARION (1887–1973) 171
ANITA LOOS (1893–1981) 175

THE SOUND ERA 181
MAE WEST (1893–1980) 181
DOROTHY PARKER (1893–1967) 186
SONYA LEVIEN (1895–1960) 189
LENORE COFFEE (1900–1984) 192
LILLIAN HELLMAN (1905–1984) 194
LEIGH BRACKETT (1915–1978) 196
HARRIET FRANK, JR. 198
JAY PRESSON ALLEN 201
FAY KANIN 203

SHORT TAKES—THE SILENTS 207
JULIA CRAWFORD IVERS (?–1930) 207
JANE MURFIN (1893–1955) 208

*SHORT TAKES—
  THE SOUND ERA* 209
FRANCES GOODRICH (1891–1984) 209
ZOË AKINS (1886–1958) 211
ELEANOR PERRY (1915–1981) 212
RUTH GORDON (1896–1985) 214

VII. ◆ Reel Women Editors

PREVIEW 219
MARGARET BOOTH (1898–) 221
VERNA FIELDS (1918–1982) 223
DEDE ALLEN 224
THELMA SCHOONMAKER 227
CAROL LITTLETON 228
SUSAN E. MORSE 230

SHORT TAKES 233
VIOLA LAWRENCE (1895–1973) 233
BARBARA MCLEAN (1909–   ) 234
ADRIENNE FAZAN (?–1965) 236

VIII. ◆ Reel Women Animators

LOTTE REINIGER (1899–1981) 241
CLAIRE PARKER (1906–1981) 243

IX. ◆ Reel Stunt Women

PREVIEW 247
PEARL WHITE (1897–1938) 249
HELEN HOLMES (1892–1950) 253
HELEN GIBSON (1894–1977) 253
HELEN THURSTON (1916–?) 254

X. ◆ "Behind Every Great Man . . ."

PREVIEW 260
JEANIE MACPHERSON (1897–1946) 261
ANNE BAUCHENS (1882–1967) 262
CLAIRE WEST (1893–1980) 264
CLARA BERANGER (1886–1956) 265
BEULAH MARIE DIX (1876–1970) 266
KAY BROWN (1903–   ) 267
JOAN HARRISON (1911–   ) 269

XI. ◆ One-of-a-kind Reel Women

PREVIEW 273
HELEN KELLER (1880–1968) 274
EDITH HEAD (1907–1981) 275
NATALIE KALMUS (1892–1965) 277
BRIANNE MURPHY 280

XII. ◆ A Reel Female Gaze /
          Select Foreign Reel
          Women

PREVIEW 285
THE SILENTS 289
GERMAINE DULAC (1882–1942) 289
MUSIDORA (1884–1957) 292

THE SOUND ERA 298
LENI RIEFENSTAHL (1902–   ) 298
MARGUERITE DURAS (1914–   ) 303
AGNES VARDA 305
MARGARETHE VON TROTTA 309
GILLIAN ARMSTRONG 313
PATRICIA ROZEMA 315
CHANTAL AKERMAN 317

SHORT TAKES—THE SILENTS 320
LEONTINE SAGAN (1889–1974) 320
ESTHER SHUB (1894–1959) 322

SHORT TAKES—
THE SOUND ERA 323
LINA WERTMULLER 323
LILIANA CAVANI 324
MAI ZETTERLING 324
DIANE KURYS 325
MÁRTA MÉSZÁROS 326

XIII. ◆ Short Takes on Other
           Unsung Reel Women

MARION FAIRFAX (1875–1970) 331
MARGARET J. WINKLER (*) 331
LOUELLA PARSONS (1893–1972) 332
HEDDA HOPPER (1890–1966) 334

Afterword 335
Select Sources 337
Notes 339
Photo Credits 363
About the Author 364
Index 365

---

* Birth and/or death dates not available. Note: Due to complaints of "ageism" by many contemporary women in the industry, birth dates not included for those still alive and working. Birth dates only included for those women still alive but no longer working.

A.A.

ACKNOWLEDGMENTS

◆ ◆ ◆

First and foremost, loving thanks to my father, Mortimer, a long-standing visionary pioneer in his own right. When I mentioned this project his first words were, "It's an idea whose time has come." My mother, Nora, typed, made photocopies, and did whatever needed to be done, lovingly, generously and, as is par for the course with great women, without ever expecting credit.

My friend and colleague, Marc Wanamaker, initially enlightened me to this subject many moons ago, generously wrote the Afterword, checked for inaccuracies, and supplied the priceless, beautiful photographs you see before you.

Tom Stempel took on the huge task of reading the first draft, and he did so with a gentle toughness and a generosity of spirit. His comments had me laughing through notes of corrections where another commentator would have left an author sobbing. Bruce Cassiday was likewise a diligent, relentless, and most careful copy editor.

Kevin Brownlow always had an ear for my questions and an encouraging word.

Thanks to Judith Crist for her invaluable comments on the first draft manuscript. Her feedback was crucial to the structural as well as to the contextual design of the book. Steve Friedman at NBC provided the initial opportunity for me to interview many of the important women included here, by asking me to produce a special segment on women behind the scenes for "The Today Show." Thanks also to NBC's Jim Brown for expertly conducting some of those interviews. Colby Atlas, in the Burbank bureau, helped faciliate all this.

Mark Hollis went beyond the call of duty many times for *Reel Women,* not the least of which was a donation of a hard disk for my computer! Miriam Hipsh provided her friendship as well as moral and financial support which allowed many of the important interviews to be conducted. Terrance Murray artfully photographed a number of the interviews for the documentary films of the same title (see About the Author), which of course translated into invaluable research for this book. I am deeply grateful to the many women in film who gave of their time to be interviewed. They know who they are. You provide great courage by your examples.

This book would not have been possible without the resources and people at the following museums and libraries: Charles Silver at the Film Studies Center at the Museum of Modern Art in New York, Madeleine Matz and Paul Spheer at the Library of Congress, Kristine Krueger, Sandra Archer, Alison Pinsler, and Sam Gill of the Margaret Herrick Library of the Academy of Motion Picture Arts and Sciences.

Thanks to all the indispensable librarians

and research people who invariably get overlooked. Ronnie Turcik of the Alice and Hamilton Fish Library in Garrison, New York who performed miracles with inter-library loans. Lori Styler did imperative last minute research with a microscopic eye.

Mabel Haddock of the National Black Programming Consortium in Columbus Ohio, and Jacquie Jones of *Black Film Review* in Washington, D.C. generously provided current information on black and third world women in film.

My kind and generous editors and friends, Michael Leach, Kyle Miller, and all the people at Continuum, who made my first book the most pleasant experience any author could hope for. Gene, Debbie, Evander, Barbara, thank you.

Thanks to The Blue Mountain Center, where much of the early research for this project was completed. A special thanks to Kaye Burnett ("The Buddha"), for her magical way of knowing and of giving without being asked. Thank you for your kindnesses and for the time I needed there.

An endless list of friends helped me to keep the big picture in perspective: my life-long friend, Donnis Newman, Margorie Bair, Judy Chaikin, Irene McKinney, and my agent, Phyllis Wender, all provided me with encouragement one step ahead by their very fine examples. I also want to thank Janis Whitney, Jolie Barbiere, John Ramo, Janis Strout (who started me touring with *Reel Women*), Magda Schoenfeld, and the Women's Spirit Group in Garrison, New York.

To all of the women I met as I traveled on lecture tour all over the United States whose words, "Thank you for doing this!" encouraged me more than they knew. This book is largely *for* and *because of* you.

The indefatigable Vanilla never had a bad word to say in all the dark nights. Van, the winter would have been a lot colder without you.

And last in this listing, but first in my life, Joan Campbell, whose tireless encouragement, support, love, not to mention expert editorial input as a writer I both respect and admire, helped me stay grounded and hopeful during the long haul. Her vision of joy and beauty assist me in more ways than she will ever know.

THE BIG HOUSE (1930), and won again for THE CHAMP (1931). (**Marion** has been quoted as writing that she saw the Oscar as "a perfect symbol of the picture business: a powerful athletic body clutching a gleaming sword with half of his head, the part which held his brains, completely sliced off.") But ask Oscar's parent Academy of Motion Picture Arts and Sciences how many other women have won Oscars and you draw a blank there and from other sources. An unofficial name count from my own record books yielded some eighty-five among the hundreds of Oscars dispensed over more than sixty years: seven other women won writing awards; ten won for film editing, five for art direction, one for set decoration, two for special effects, one for choreography, seven for music, eighteen for documentaries and short films, and there were thirty-two Oscars awarded to women for costume design, of which seven went to **Edith Head,** five to **Irene Sharaff,** and two apiece to **Helen Rose** and **Dorothy Jeakins.**

It's also difficult to get a head count from the guilds. The Directors Guild of America, which has taken the lead in trying to increase the number of women and minorities in the industry, reports a continuing growth thereof but the figure is still only at 18 percent, some 1,620 of its 9,000 members. Women constitute 13 percent of the production managers; 23 percent of the first assistant directors; 33 percent of the second assistant directors; 38 percent of the associate directors in tape, and 23 percent of the stage managers. The Producers Guild of America reports that 50 of its 416 active and inactive members are women and that there's been steady growth in their numbers in recent years. The Writers Guild of America reports that 38 percent, some 3,914 of its 10,300 members are women, but this includes those who write for both television and film or television exclusively, as well as newswriters. There's no breakdown of screenwriters.

All this underlines the importance of Ally's work, indeed an archeological survey as well as a sociological, cultural, and feminist study. Its virtue is that it is not the definitive encyclopedia of women in film: it is a personal and passionate work that will, I know, inspire others. Welcome.

—Judith Crist